T0316467

THE VICTORIAN AGE
IN POLITICS, WAR
AND DIPLOMACY

THE VICTORIAN AGE IN POLITICS, WAR AND DIPLOMACY

by

HAROLD TEMPERLEY,

M.A., LITT.D., F.B.A.

Reader in Modern History in the University of Cambridge

THE

INAUGURAL LECTURE

UNIVERSITY OF CAMBRIDGE

LOCAL LECTURES SUMMER

MEETING 1928

CAMBRIDGE

AT THE UNIVERSITY PRESS

1928

CAMBRIDGE
UNIVERSITY PRESS

University Printing House, Cambridge CB2 8BS, United Kingdom

Cambridge University Press is part of the University of Cambridge.

It furthers the University's mission by disseminating knowledge in the pursuit of education, learning and research at the highest international levels of excellence.

www.cambridge.org
Information on this title: www.cambridge.org/9781107536913

© Cambridge University Press 1928

First published 1928
Re-issued 2015

A catalogue record for this publication is available from the British Library

ISBN 978-1-107-53691-3 Paperback

THE VICTORIAN AGE
IN POLITICS, WAR
AND DIPLOMACY

I

IF my definition confines the Victorian
Age to politics, to arms, and to diplomacy it is not only because limitation
leads to clearness. It is because in these
three departments there is, I believe, less
revision to be done by posterity than
elsewhere. In the realms of culture and
art for instance some of the Victorian
gods have sunk into demigods or been
degraded to the condition of mere mortal
men. To mention a few names at ran-
dom, Lord Lytton and Lord Leighton
have suffered the doom of too much
applause, and figures like Matthew Arnold

and Swinburne, George Eliot and even Tennyson are noticeably diminished in size. In philosophy there is the same tale. Herbert Spencer has vanished beneath a horizon towards which Stuart Mill is slowly sinking. Even in science, where the greatest results were achieved, the discoveries acclaimed in the Victorian Age are not always regarded as final. To take one instance, while the *Origin of Species* was overthrowing political, religious and scientific conceptions everywhere, an obscure monk was meditating among his peas and his beehives in a forgotten abbey in Czecho-Slovakia. The theories of Abbot Mendel, published in an obscure journal—and not appreciated by the world until 1900, are perhaps to-day as penetrating and vital as those of Darwin. And that is a significant comment on the complacency of the Victorian Era, and on its profound belief that its great men, or at least those whom it thought its great men, had solved all problems and revealed all secrets worth knowing.

II

About the leaders of culture, of science and of thought then in this age opinions still waver, and there are verdicts which may yet be reversed. But warriors, statesmen and diplomats are brought to rough and practical tests in their own time, and are therefore more easily assayed by posterity. Among parliamentarians (reckoning Lord Palmerston and Lord Salisbury as diplomats) four at least were in the first rank. At the beginning of the reign Sir Robert Peel marshalled a dazzling array of talents to atone for a lack of genius. Towards its close Joseph Chamberlain displayed an imagination and energy which are not easily paralleled in our history. In Gladstone the Victorian age found, in the opinion of a still living statesman, the first of all Parliamentarians. And, whether we follow the dazzling intricacies of his policy in his biography, or merely gaze with the poet on 'the arcane face of the much-wrinkled Jew,' we shall not deny the authentic marks of genius to Disraeli.

Milton's account of the debate of fiends in hell, under the presidency of Satan, is said to have trained the Elder Pitt for his work in the Commons. You, more fortunate than he, can view (not I hope in a presidential capacity) every turn of fence in that famed series of oratorical duels between Gladstone and Disraeli and compare them with those in which the younger Pitt engaged with Fox and Canning with Brougham. A cursory reading of these speeches will in each case assign the palm to the most literary efforts—to those of Pitt, Canning and Disraeli. But a more careful study will reveal in the less adorned words of their rivals some of that debating superiority which renders an argument irresistible for one moment of time and unreadable for the rest of eternity.

There were great men indeed in the Victorian Age, yet the movements were greater than the men, which means that the common man, the man in the counting-house or in the shop, was the greatest man of all. Institutions, laws, ideas, movements obeyed his behest or were moulded in his image. It was the age of an emancipated and emancipating middle-class, a precise age, a complacent age, which sincerely depreciated all preceding ages. A poet has pictured a great writer (whose name I suppress because he was also a historian) as the Emperor of this bourgeois Olympus, satirising other times in comparison with his own, 'pointing out how much things had improved since the days when the gods were unbreeched savages, content with a monotonous diet of ambrosia, and drinking doubtful nectar in place of [Victorian] Madeira[1].' To-day at least we cannot think that the London of the Great Exhibition of 1851 had a conspicuous superiority over the Queen of the Adriatic or the City of the Violet Crown.

III

Of all political developments—except one—the greatest was in that of the prestige of the sovereign. Everyone knows I think that Queen Victoria adopted the title of Empress after a reign of forty years. Does anyone know that George the Third refused to accept it after reigning the same period ? Here is the evidence in a diplomatic despatch of Canning's in 1825. 'His late Majesty George III was advised at the time of the Union with Ireland in compensation for His Majesty's abandonment, then

[1] Francis Thompson (1902), *Works*, III. 223.

voluntarily made of the Title of King of France, which had been so long annexed to the Crown of England, to assume the title of Emperor of the British and Hanoverian Dominions; but His late Majesty felt that His true dignity consisted in His being known to Europe and the World, by the appropriated and undisputed style belonging to the British Crown[1].' Is it not evident that when Queen Victoria accepted what George the Third had refused, she was displaying a type of monarchy more self-confident, more consciously splendid, and more definitely desirous, as Disraeli said, of operating on the minds and imaginations of her subjects, and particularly of her Oriental subjects?

But it was not only this carefully staged appeal that moved the hearts of subjects. Monarchy arose from its ashes

[1] Stapleton's *Political Life of Canning* [1831], II. 361-2 *note*.

under Victoria. George the Fourth, chiefly through the scandals of his Royal Divorce Bill, had endangered his dynasty as well as his throne. On his death, *The Times* criticised the late monarch, adding that they had 'not floated down the putrid stream of flattery.' Peel exclaimed that he did not think the Monarchy could last more than five or six years. William the Fourth indeed did something to regain the lost popularity of the Monarchy, but Greville tells us how the young Queen appeared in public early in her reign on one occasion, and that no one raised a hat or a cheer. Can we imagine any such welcome to royalty as possible nowadays?

One reason of royal unpopularity was undoubtedly the active attempt of the third and fourth George to intervene personally in politics. A more subtle cause was the old Whig theory of the revolution which regarded resistance to the Crown as a glorious duty in 1688 and desired to make the King of England as powerless as the Doge of Venice. This tradition of putting the sovereign in her place plainly inspired Lord Palmerston in his notorious struggle with the Crown. And Lord John Russell, whom Queen Victoria at length induced to dismiss Lord Palmerston, reminded that lady on a later occasion that revolution was the origin of the present form of Government and dynasty. The tradition of 1688, you see, died slowly and hard.

IV

An increase in the Empire has usually meant an increase in the popularity of the Crown. Certainly as dominions scatter and increase the only binding link is the broad gold circle of the Crown, and the only possible head is the crowned head. General Smuts pointed out that an elective ruler in a hetero-

geneous empire, comprising self-governing democracies, is an impossibility.
A hereditary ruler prevents contested
elections and represents in historic, visible
and majestic strength the only permanent
symbol of imperial unity.

During the first years of Victoria's
reign the colonies were seething with
unrest; Frenchmen were in revolt in
Canada, Englishmen in Jamaica, Boers
had seceded from Cape Colony, and
mutinous convicts were being trans-
ported to Australia. New Zealand alone
was tranquil perhaps because British
settlement was just beginning there.
During the next sixty years all except
one of these turbulent democracies settled
down quietly beneath the sway of the
Crown, and the Home Government
finally reduced that one to submission
by the aid of all the others. The secret
of harmony is to be found in Durham's
famous report on Responsible Govern-

ment. He recommended that the Executive in a colony should be made to depend on the will of the majority of the popular house, and with this key he unlocked the hearts of the colonists. He found 'Collision between the Executive and representative body.' He created the tradition that a working identity of will and interest between Executive and Legislative was 'the natural state of government in all colonies.' Durham himself claimed that he was applying to the colonies overseas a principle established in England herself by the Revolution of 1688[1] though others have discovered Radical influences in his ideals. In reality the substance of his policy had been stated by Fox in the debate on Canada in 1791 when he laid down that 'the only method of retaining distant colonies with advantage was to enable them to govern themselves.'

1 Durham, *Report* of 1839 (1902), pp. 51, 55.

Perhaps it was fortunate for the Colonies that neither Durham nor the Home Government understood the full logic of his principles. Durham himself reserved to the Home Government the control of trade, of defence, and of imperial interests. We owe it not to Durham but to the doctrine of Free Trade and to the readiness of the Colonies to assume military burdens, that their self-government became complete. It came as a painful shock to the Mother Country when Canada imposed a protective tariff against England in 1859, and when her Minister of Commerce replied to the maternal protest in language remarkable for its strength. The views and pretensions of the Mother Country were compared to those 'of a provincial town ...professedly actuated by selfish motives.' 'Self-government,' it was added, 'would be utterly annihilated if the views of the Imperial Government were to be pre-

ferred to those of the people of Canada [1].'
This sharp rebuke together with Canada's
protective tariff were accepted by the
Mother Country with meekness. The
episode should not be deemed humilia-
ting but glorious. Is it not the best
example to be found of the union of
what Disraeli, in a famous speech, called
'Imperium et Libertas'[2]? Is it not, in
Bolingbroke's phrase, 'the temper of a
government in which things so seldom
allied as Empire and Liberty are in-

[1] Sir A. T. Galt, Canadian Finance Minister to
the Colonial Secretary, *Accounts and Papers* (1864),
XLI. pp. 11–12.

[2] The phrase is used by Tacitus of the Emperor
Nerva, and was repeated by Clarendon and Bolingbroke, from the last of whom Disraeli probably
derived it. The Bolingbroke quotations are from
the *Patriot King*. The speech of Disraeli of 24th June
1872 is brilliantly imaginative but it suggests restric-
tions on the powers of Colonies, to which they could
hardly have submitted. The speech of Gladstone in
the Commons of 26th April 1870 is worth reading
by way of contrast.

timately mixed, co-exist together inseparably, and constitute one real essence'? Is not this 'asserting triumphantly the right and the honour of Great Britain, as far as waters roll and as winds can waft them'?

It is not, of course, the fact that our troubles with our overseas possessions ended in 1859 because rough words came from Ottawa and soft answers were returned from Downing Street. Even so late as 1873 Gladstone, as much the champion of *libertas* as Disraeli was of *imperium*, sorely resented the resolve of the Australian colonies to manage their own commercial tariffs, and in such a way that 'no treaty entered into by the Imperial Government should in any way limit or impede the exercise of such right.' He gave way with regret for he still thought the Empire a unit and wished to prevent too great a separation of its parts. Yet this diversity in unity is the peculiar characteristic of the British Empire, which is the most various and flexible of all political forms. The Roman Empire perished because of its unity and rigidity, because, as Coleridge said, the Imperial idea overlaid and destroyed the national one. The British Empire survives because it has become multicellular, because each part as it separates develops a self-sufficing life of its own. To-day the centre of the Empire lies not only in London, but in Ottawa, in Cape Town, in Canberra, in Wellington, perhaps even in Dublin and in Delhi. And its vitality is assured so long as the Dominions regard the Empire as existing, not in order to enforce authority, but to promote liberty.

The method by which colonies, once disaffected or rebellious, were reconciled and retained seems the great contribution of the Victorian age to political science. Its application is even now refused to those vast domains along the tropic belt that we know as the Crown Colonies and Dependencies. And from two great areas the Victorian statesmen withheld the precious boon altogether. Ireland— the scene of such tragedy—found little solace from her sorrows during the reign. India—as a result of mutiny and war— freed herself from John Company and was elevated by Disraeli into an Empire. But this at least was an Empire to which no one thought of giving liberty. Even under Edward VII the philosopher, who ruled India from Whitehall, never dreamed that she could be governed by her own parliament or people. 'So far as my imagination extends,' said Lord Morley, India would remain an auto- cracy. One imperial Amurath would follow another as in the immemorial past. Fortune banters the philosopher when he tries to be a political prophet. Within ten years of this utterance another Secretary of State promised India that she should receive Responsible and Parliamentary Government.

V

To domestic, as distinguished from Imperial, politics and legislation the Victorian Age made no strikingly original contribution. There were great advances indeed but along lines already indicated. Canning and Huskisson had initiated scientific legislation of the modern type, and the Whig Ministry of Grey had reformed the heart and the head as well as the members. They had not feared to lay hands on the Ark of the Constitution, and to attack that ancient citadel of privilege, the parliamentary franchise itself. Therefore the tradition which they established was one of destruction of privilege—religious and aristocratic. They were, of course, denounced as revolutionaries, and Sir Archibald Alison pictured the demons of hell exulting at their triumph. But they were neither as diabolical nor even as revolutionary as they seemed. They destroyed an old machinery in 1832, and produced a new model franchise which they hoped would give power to the middle class and restrain democratic excesses for two or three generations. But according to Disraeli the passing of the Reform Bill was like the eating of the forbidden fruit by Adam and Eve. It taught us that we were naked and the shame of democracy followed as a matter of course. Yet, if democracy was inevitable after 1832, the movement towards it was strangely faltering and slow. The delay was due, I think, to a very curious fact and to a very curious man. A real and new freedom—freedom of opinion—now existed; a real and new method of expressing opinions—by agitation at public meetings outside the walls of parliament

—may I call it extra-mural agitation?—
had just been discovered. Popular agitation had abolished slavery and carried
the Reform Bill to victory. It was
used as the most convenient of political
weapons under Victoria, most notably
in Cobden's agitation for abolishing the
Corn-Laws. If the popular will could
prevail in this way there was less need
for the vote and the ballot-box. Then
there was the press, which developed
and reacted upon public opinion, and
there was Lord Palmerston who used
both for his own purposes. And this
statesman—the idol of cheap newspapers
and the favourite of the crowd—steadily
opposed any Parliamentary reform. The
people acquiesced during his lifetime
in this drag on the electoral wheel.
Immediately after his death a democratic
franchise was extended to the boroughs,
and, within half a generation, to the
counties. It is singular that there was

no serious attempt to extend it to women. No woman was considered fit to exercise a vote in a reign when a woman was considered fit to rule three hundred millions of subjects.

The privilege of descent had conferred power on the Peers, as on the Queen. They felt weak at her accession, for they had opposed the Reform Bill and had been overthrown like the Titans. But their humiliation was more apparent than real, and their share in the government was considerable. Of Victoria's ten prime ministers six were peers by birth, two became so by creation, and two only remained Commoners. In every Cabinet of the reign there was a majority of peers and peers' sons over Commoners until Gladstone's Second Ministry of 1880. The Lords shewed judicious moderation for a long time in dealing with the Commons. And even when they came to sharp passages of arms with Gladstone, they either chose their ground for resistance well or abandoned it before the situation became critical. They shewed a truly bourgeois moderation and avoided all conflicts, such as that under the Budget of 1909, likely to result in a legislative limitation of power. The changes in their composition and social status are interesting. Some of the peers renewed their blood and restored their fortunes with the inexhaustible virgin wealth of the United States. And they began to be recruited from the plutocracy in the year 1880 which thus witnessed a change in the House of Lords as well as in the Cabinet. In that year great accessions to its numbers began. During two-thirds of Victoria's reign the increase to the peerage had been slight. During her last twenty years batches of peers—like fresh-baked loaves—were turned out at the regular rate of some nine a year, giving a total of nearly two hundred. Either the merit of aspirants or the perception of premiers must have greatly increased. And this singular alteration in the laws of demand and supply forms an interesting subject of inquiry both to economist and to politician.

Far more important were the changes in the Commons. The power of its leader increased and he tended to become the effective ruler, even when his nominal chief sat in the Lords. As members of the Commons remained unpaid, a monetary qualification existed which made it difficult for a poor man to be a member, and thus hindered the formation of a Parliamentary Labour party. The dualistic party system, the characteristic English form, remained, though the Peelite, the Irish and the fourth parties at times threatened to disturb it. There were important changes in machinery. The growth of political organisation outside parliament tended to give power to its leaders and to destroy the independence of their followers. It is often stated (and sometimes believed) that the Cabinet forms the executive, and the Commons the legislative, government of this country. During the Victorian age there was a reversal of these parts. About 1850 the development of the system of parliamentary questions in its modern form, gave to the individual member a new and genuine control over the executive. This system of detailed and precise inquiry enables acute or laborious private members to supervise the administrative departments of state if not altogether, yet in many important directions. It is a most effective control over the Civil Service (in itself a creation of the reign), that silent almost invincible army, which lends all ministers its invisible support. By contrast, and as if in revenge, the Cabinet has become the chief, if not the sole, legislating agency. When the

Cabinet in effect initiates most legislation, the Commons find it difficult to oppose them. The tendency was long resisted under Victoria and private members like Lord Ashley or Sir John Lubbock (Lord Avebury) maintained their independence of the Cabinet and passed important bills into law. But after 1880 such achievements were few, and the institution of the gag and of the closure limited freedom of debate and exalted the supremacy of the Cabinet. Legislation became in fact the chief occupation of executive ministers, the standard by which they rose and fell, the index of their activity and popularity. We are far indeed from the days of the Elder Pitt. The Great Commoner made no important addition to the Statute Book, yet he was the choice and the darling of the people.

It was Lecky who praised the period between the passing of the Reform Bill and the death of Palmerston. He says that all classes were represented in the parliament and that we never had a better government. This is a judgment rather according to faith than according to works. The representation of all classes does not always produce such legislation as the majority desires or even such as it earnestly needs. There can be no doubt that laws abolishing privilege or providing means of self-help were eagerly passed. Such measures were the removal of Jewish disabilities, the disestablishment of the Irish Church, the opening of the Universities to Catholics and Dissenters. Admirable again, at least in intention, were the institution of promotion by merit in the military, naval, and civil services, the abolition of the Corn Duties and the simplification of the Tariff. But while such movements generally succeeded, a demand for change in conditions of life, such as was made by the Chartist movement, generally failed. The Poor Law was conceived and administered under a harsh theory, sanitation and nursing conditions were neglected. The history of Lord Shaftesbury's noble and ultimately successful efforts to prevent tiny children and women working in factories or mines under indescribable conditions is a sad one. The governments of the time were not exactly hostile, but they were unenthusiastic. And the opposition by theoretical advocates of the 'dismal science,' and by practical champions of their own interests, make painful reading even today. Shaftesbury ascribed his ultimate victory to a majority in the Commons which was actuated not by love of his cause but by hatred of Sir Robert Peel. Hatred has seldom been more useful, but after all it is not the permanent driving force behind humane legislation. The Victorian record on Education is also most unsatisfactory. It was not until

1870 that an Elementary Education Act was passed in England, a measure already long operative in almost every other country in Europe. It may be admitted here that the chief cause of this shameful delay was not political inertia but religious dissension. Even this excuse could not be pleaded for the delay in producing satisfactory laws dealing with combinations of labourers. It was not until 1875 that Disraeli, by a sound piece of constructive work, settled this question for a generation.

In fairness to our Victorians it should be conceded that negative work may have to precede positive legislation. The wilderness must be cleared before the settler can erect his log-cabin. None the less the age of self-help favoured individual at the expense of collective enterprise. It was horrified at Bismarck's disregard for Parliament, but still more horrified at his bold experiments in State

Socialism, experiments which have long since been adopted by England herself.

After all in that age one can understand Ruskin's indignation against a political economy founded on self-interest. One can understand too his passionate exclamation 'THERE IS NO WEALTH BUT LIFE!'

VI

An age can hardly be called enlightened, which acts negligently if not cruelly towards those who, in the most literal sense, spend their lives in its service. And this age was as callous in its treatment of the soldier as it was humane in its treatment of the slave. The soldier was lodged in barracks where the confined space and the infamous sanitation subjected him to suffering and to disease. He was crammed or 'hutted' for sleep into a wooden crib which he actually had to share with three comrades even during the torrid nights of the tropics.

Not until 1827 did the Duke of Wellington succeed in procuring each soldier a single bed and an iron bedstead. The gain in cleanliness and health (as we can readily believe) was reported as very great[1]. But reform stopped there. When the soldier fought in the tropics he wore a tight jacket and a leather stock, ate salt beef and drank rum, and often fell a helpless victim to disease. Sir John Moore had aimed at the moral elevation of the soldier; a goal which the Iron Duke regarded as unattainable. The soldier, he wrote officially in 1829, is 'in general the most drunken and probably the worst man of the trade or profession to which he belongs or of the village or town in which he lives[2].' His only remedies lay in a wooden drill

1 *Hans. Deb.* N.S. xvi. p. 562. Sir H. Hardinge in the Commons.

2 Wellington, *Despatches, Correspondence and Memoranda* [1873], v. p. 594.

and an iron discipline, maintained by flogging from which he did not exempt the women attached to the army. Humanity appeared in the army only after the horrors of the Crimean War. The married British soldier was at length rescued from horrible conditions by the provision of separate quarters for his wife and children. Lord Wolseley says this reform was due to the Prince Consort and adds '[previously] we were forced to ignore those ordinary decencies of life which are usually respected even among savages.' Humanity owes an even deeper debt to Florence Nightingale not only in the army but in every quarter where the State has marshalled the aid of science to alleviate suffering or to fight disease.

The age treated the first captain in Europe almost as badly as it treated his soldiers. Cromwell had been strong enough to preserve his army when war was over; Wellington, like Marlborough, witnessed an almost total destruction of the splendid force he had created and led. He could do nothing but yield to the times. He broke up his military staff, he sacrificed the subsidiary services, he disbanded the Militia. He saved the Yeomanry by urging that they were a police force. He saved a number of regular regiments by sending them abroad and hiding them in holes and corners of the Empire. For the redcoats could only be maintained in strength when they were hidden from sight by a thousand leagues of blue water. The arrangement injured both public and army. Expense was doubled, for it cost twice as much to keep a man in the tropics. Security was halved because seventy thousand men dotted the circumference of the Empire while a few poor thousands defended its heart. Wolseley says that, if the French had landed in force in 1837, London must have fallen before them. The Duke himself emphasised our defenceless state in 1847. At first he found only Palmerston to support, or even to understand, him, but their combined vigour effected some reforms and only just in time. An increase took place in the field artillery, and the Militia was raised from the dead, and without the Militia, as was seen very soon, the Crimean War could hardly have been fought. The avoidable losses and hideous scandals of that war strengthened the hands of military reformers. Palmerston swept away the old conflicting authorities and concentrated control under a new Secretary of State for War —with the General Commanding-in-Chief as a military adviser. He further reorganised the Militia and produced an elaborate if not wholly successful system of coast defence. The Prince Consort persuaded Palmerston to arm the troops with a breech-loading rifle, and drafted the regulations for the new Volunteer Force. This volunteer movement had deep social and political roots, and evoked a curious corresponding movement in the Colonies. It coincided with the development of compulsory military service in Europe, and was indeed a British and Colonial gesture of defiance to it. Together with the Militia the Volunteers provided a second line of defence, and gave a margin of safety to the country which it had not hitherto possessed. The work was completed by Lord Cardwell, who abolished purchase of commissions, linked up overseas battalions with the home forces, and created a reserve. Parliament was, for once, sympathetic for he worked under the shadow of the Prussian military triumphs of 1870. But the army was still defective. It was still in the elementary or garrison and regimental stage. Staff officers were now trained but there was still no General

37

Staff, and no effective brain to the Army. Plans of defence were inadequate, and there was no scheme for sending effective forces overseas, still less for maintaining them at strength during a great war. And the war in South Africa, though it proved we had learned something since the Crimea, revealed our military weakness at the close of the reign.

During the whole of this period our Navy ruled the waves. But the Navy alone does not confer safety. Our sailors could not promise to prevent a foreign force from landing on our shores, they could only promise to prevent it from leaving them. For land-defence therefore military garrisons were needed not only in England but also in many other parts of the Empire. In India the Mutiny caused a thorough reorganisation of the Anglo-Indian Army, and this force was maintained at strength. But the position in the Colonies had altered. Since the loss of America the Mother Country had demanded a rigid obedience in return for effective military protection. But the granting of Colonial self-government caused the Home Government to reconsider their military policy. A reversion was attempted to the old eighteenth-century system whereby the Mother Country gave some military aid and left the Colonies to furnish the rest. This scheme was condemned first by history and next by recent practice. It was, said Gladstone, an 'invention, of which up to the present time we are the patentees, and no one has shewn a disposition to invade our patent.' It produced a dangerous reduction of imperial garrisons without an increase of colonial forces sufficient to fill the gap and to ensure safety. One witness at the Select Committee of inquiry in 1861 said, 'Every [imperial] soldier in a colony prevents a hundred colonists from taking arms and drilling.'

The situation revealed in 1861 was indeed extraordinary. The Empire (excluding India) was defended by about 42,000 imperial troops and by about 20,000 colonial ones. England spent three millions yearly on colonial defence, the Colonies themselves about one-eighth of that amount. Since 1814 nearly two million pounds had been spent in fortifying the Bahamas (which were quite unimportant) and many millions elsewhere, but none of the fortifications were even in a tolerable state of defence except in the Mediterranean. One ex-Colonial Secretary (who was supported by an admiral and the existing Secretary of State for War) stated that, with a few exceptions, almost the whole of this immense amount of money spent on fortifications had been absolutely wasted 'and the wisest thing we could do now would be to blow them up again[1].'

1 Earl Grey, *Accounts and Papers*, XIII [1861],

These vigorous utterances at least blew away a good many current misconceptions and led to the adoption of sound though rudimentary principles of defence. In future it was decided to make the Colonies primarily responsible for their own defence by means of their own local forces. The Mother Country undertook to defend them by sea-power and retained special control over certain places even in self-governing colonies, like the Virgin Fortress of Halifax. Most of the imperial troops were withdrawn from the self-governing colonies early in the seventies and concentrated at home 'as it is the tendency of modern warfare to strike blows at the heart of a hostile power.' The problem of naval defence was hardly as yet touched. And, though contributions were occasionally made to it by separate colonies, the Navy

p.155, for other important details cf. pp. 119, 130–1, 207, 309–11, 333.

remained under the Mother Country's control.

This inquiry throws a strong light upon the whole nature of colonial sentiment in the sixties. Gladstone only expressed the underlying thought of the more enlightened. 'The privileges of freedom and the burdens of freedom are absolutely associated together; to bear the burdens is as necessary as to enjoy the privileges[1].' And again, 'I do not think self-government entire and genuine in any case where it is not connected with very large responsibility for self-defence.' The Colonies proved to be quite as ready to defend, as to govern, themselves. During the seventies English ministers encouraged the federal idea in South Africa and Australasia, but neither Disraeli nor Gladstone committed themselves to the idea of federation of the empire as a whole. Disraeli, though

1 *Accounts and Papers*, XIII [1861], pp. 349, 360.

preoccupied with our Eastern Empire, shewed a desire to attract the sympathies of self-governing colonies. And he appointed both a Colonial Defence Committee and a Royal Commission during the years 1878–9 to inquire into the defence of British possessions and commerce abroad. These did not in the end produce much result but a remarkable proposal was made at the Colonial Conference of 1887 by the delegates from Cape Colony. They suggested 'the feasibility of promoting closer union between the different parts of the Empire by means of an Imperial Customs' tariff [say two per cent. upon all foreign produce imported into the United Kingdom and the Colonies], the revenue derived from such tariff to be devoted to the general defence of the Empire.' This proposal was ably urged by Mr Hofmeyr and met with support from other colonies but the English statesmen shewed no disposition even to discuss it[1]. One would like to know the secret of their silence.

During the eighties Lord Rosebery had touched the idea of imperial federation, and Chamberlain gave a new meaning to the sentiment of Empire in the nineties. But sentiment had to supply the place of plan and forethought. There was no scheme of war coordinated between Mother Country and Colonies. 'The question of imperial defence,' says a brilliant military writer, 'had never been approached from the standpoint of imperial strategy.' In the moment of danger colonies offered the local levies they had raised to the Mother Country for the defence of the Empire. After the South African War in 1902 Chamberlain pointed out to Colonial Premiers that the Mother Country bore a burden

1 *Accounts and Papers*, LVI [1887], pp. 477–83, 586–7.

nine times greater per head of population than that paid by any colony. He obtained some smallish contributions to the Imperial navy, but the main expense and all the responsibility for the defence of the Empire remained with the Mother Country. It is clear that, so far as the Colonies were concerned, the problem of defence had not moved forward much since 1861. And the later development of Chamberlain's schemes for Imperial unity lie outside the Victorian Age.

VII

Experts have long disputed as to whether armaments depend upon policy or policy upon armaments. In the Victorian age the answer seems easy enough. The navy was effective sometimes, as for instance in protecting Constantinople, but its power was purely defensive. We had no permanent allies in Europe and no aggressive weapons to use against our enemies. Wellington believed that our policy should be pacific because our army was in no condition to fight anyone. Palmerston knew this as well as the Duke, and, when defying other powers, relied either on a military ally or on his ability to stir up political unrest in the other country. Somebody says 'a Foreign Office is only the façade of a War Office.' But the Foreign Office had no such support between Waterloo and the Crimean War, and these years witnessed a long series of diplomatic triumphs.

The two greatest figures in modern British diplomacy fell short of the Victorian era. They are quoted as representing alternative policies. Castlereagh made friends with despots, promoted international congresses and movements, and figures as the good European. Canning defied foreign despots, dissolved their conclaves, and is asserted to have championed national liberty in the name of England. These generalisations are too sharp. Castlereagh wrote of the 'old and poisoned system' of European diplomacy, and was a patriotic Englishman in his own way. Canning thought we could not withdraw from Europe, and worked with one despot to emancipate Latin America and with another to liberate Greece. But there was one real difference between them; Castlereagh ignored public opinion and failed, Canning lived by it and succeeded. Even if Canning had not wanted to be English, public opinion would not have permitted him to be European.

England was not, as such, opposed to European Congresses. Canning indeed laid down the conditions on which England would join them. A Congress, he said, must avow beforehand that it would not intervene in the internal affairs of other states; small powers as well as great must be represented there;

no power, great or small, must sit 'as a judge in a cause in which she was a party'; the seat of discussion must be a small town or neutral capital. As the despots of Europe refused these terms, Canning refused to meet them in Congress. Soon after his death revolutions occurred, the Great Powers accepted most of Canning's principles, and a new Congress met and sat for several years. The chief result of its sessions was that 'scrap of paper' treaty which gave Belgium independence and life. Canning's ideas of a European Congress are of even more interest to-day than in 1830. For they have been incorporated, with almost literal exactness, into the Constitution of that League of Nations, which meets at the 'small and neutral' town of Geneva.

To Palmerston, who almost monopolised foreign policy during the first half of the reign, the epithet of 'entirely English' might be more truly applied

than to Canning. He kept a bust of
Canning in his study and had it painted
in the background of his own portrait. But
his imitation of the master was one of
trick and effect rather than of likeness.
Palmerston believed in settling each question on its individual merits, Canning
in a system based on real intellectual
principles. Palmerston said he adopted
Canning's phrase that England's interests
were the Shibboleth of his policy. But
the two men differed as to what England's
interests were. Canning said it was 'not
a British interest to have free states established on the Continent[1],' Palmerston
thought it our interest to establish and
maintain free states in Greece, Portugal,
Spain and Italy. Canning wanted to be
'an umpire' in the conflict between
despots and free states; Palmerston declared that the free states were 'our
natural allies.' Canning wrote 'A menace,

1 My *Foreign Policy of Canning* [1925], p. 458.

which is not intended to be executed is an engine which Great Britain should never condescend to employ.' Palmerston employed the engine of menace with extraordinary success for thirty years, till in his old age he shattered it and his reputation on the iron that was Bismarck.

There were good things as well as bad in Palmerston's diplomacy. If he sometimes disregarded Europe he did not usually disregard humanity. In one of his most Victorian efforts he declared that England alone felt 'a deep and sincere interest' in abolishing the Slave Trade, and that we alone kept all other nations to their agreements about it. The despots of Europe imagined that they 'could keep down opinion by force of arms.' Palmerston thought and said that such repression could only end in revolution. It may have been tactless to say so, for diplomatists do not like to find a prophet, or even a lecturer, in their midst. But in the year 1848 every despot in Europe, except the Czar, ran away from his capital to escape the anger of his people. Constitutional England remained quiet, so Europe thought Palmerston might be right after all.

Palmerston had a sympathy with other nationalities, as well as his own, at least when they were struggling towards freedom. He sometimes controlled this sympathy in deference to England's interests. Thus he insisted on retaining Servia beneath the Turkish yoke and left Hungary to be subdued by Austria, in each case to preserve the Balance of Power. But the best aspects of his policy were shewn when he joined with his old opponent, Lord John Russell, to smoothe the path and welcome the achievement of Italian unity, a service which made Garibaldi exclaim 'the English have been the friends of freedom all the world over.' Less defensible is his more narrowly national side, the policy expressed in the notorious words *Ciuis Britannicus sum*'; a policy vaunting, aggressive, egoistic, displayed oftenest to small States who could not resent it or to large States who had small navies. Yet—even here—there was a good side. Quotations from two speeches will express both the defects and the merits of this attitude. Here we have an almost purely Chauvinistic note. 'I confess also it [the adoption of the principle of settling disputes by arbitration] would be a very dangerous course for this country itself to take, because there is no country which from its political and commercial circumstances, from its maritime interests, and from its colonial possessions, excites more envious and jealous feelings in different quarters than England does; and there is no country that would find it more difficult to discover really disinterested and impartial arbiters' (June 12, 1849).

Again, 'England is sincerely desirous to preserve and maintain peace...but it is essential...that it should be well known and understood by every nation on the face of the earth that we are not disposed to submit to wrong, and that the maintenance of peace on our part is subject to the indispensable condition that all countries shall respect our honour and our dignity, and shall not inflict any injury upon our interests.' And here is the highest note he ever reached: 'Opinions are stronger than armies. Opinions, if they are founded in truth and justice, will in the end prevail against the bayonets of infantry, the fire of artillery, and the charge of cavalry. Therefore, I say, that armed by opinion, if that opinion is pronounced with truth and justice, we are indeed strong, and in the end likely to make that opinion prevail[1].'

1 Both the latter quotations are from a speech of July 21, 1849. *Hans. Deb.* 3rd Ser. CVII. pp. 813–4.

A personality so strong as Palmerston, with a policy so vigorous and so unconventional, was bound to provoke a reaction against both in a free country. Nationalism is supposed to be the child of the middle class, but in England internationalism proved to be its twin. A curious movement denouncing the false glories of war, preaching non-intervention and a commercial freedom as the means of international peace, originated with Cobden and with Bright. It was attuned to the mind of the business man. 'The middle and industrious classes of England can have no interest apart from the preservation of peace.' 'Free Trade was the international law of God Almighty.' By following the path of peaceful industry England would attain far greater moral and physical power than Russia can hope to reach by 'the opposite career of war and conquest.' Then came the Crimean War, which stigmatised Russia as the power of evil and Bright and Cobden as traitors. But the vain sufferings of the war, its trifling results, and finally our diplomatic humiliations before Bismarck produced a revulsion of public feeling. Even a Conservative like the future Lord Salisbury preferred the policy of Cobden to that of Palmerston. We would then have contracted no contracts we dishonoured and uttered no boasts we did not fulfil. And the tide went on rising till it lapped the feet of that 'foul idol' before which Palmerston had so often bowed, the idol of the 'Balance of Power.' The phrase appeared in twenty treaties of the period as the object of their agreement; it came before Parliament every year in a clause of the Mutiny Act. For thirty years Cobden and John Bright had declared it to be a delusion; at length it was expunged from the Mutiny Act in 1868. This was the high-water mark of what was called—somewhat cruelly—the 'calico millennium' proclaimed by 'a bagman.'

Business men are not in fact sure guides in diplomacy, and Cobden's doctrine of non-intervention in Europe and of no defence except the navy was unreal and academic. But Gladstone, who at length became Prime Minister, had remoulded the ideas in a religious crucible and was prepared with a foreign policy halfway between Cobdenite and Palmerstonian extremes. Bismarck was now at the height of his strength—the age was of 'Blood and Iron' and not friendly to Gladstone's doctrine that right was might, or that force lay in law. Yet he had some success. He caused France and Germany alike to endorse the neutrality of Belgium in 1870, he got Russia to attend a conference which released her (instead of allowing her to release herself) from onerous clauses in the Treaty of 1856. And he crowned his work by the Arbitration Settlement whereby the British Government paid three million pounds to the United States for the damages done by the *Alabama*. We have seen how Palmerston denounced arbitration, though in fact it had already settled some of our difficulties. But this striking example was a step forward towards ' a law which favours the pacific, not the bloody settlement of disputes, which aims at permanent and not temporary adjustments; above all, which recognises, as a tribunal of paramount authority, the general judgment of civilised mankind.'

Yet the Victorian Age was not to close in a Gladstonian dream of peace and arbitration. Disraeli replaced him in power and was prepared with a new foreign policy, or rather perhaps with an old one. While he was Prime Minister he read his former novels not for amusement but for instruction. And his dreams of romance were to become the realities of statesmanship. For he found a complete programme of policy in the East in the fantastic pages of *Tancred*. The hero and the Arab sheikhs, with whom he consorts, suggest that Queen Victoria will become Empress of India and that England will one day add Cyprus to her dominions. They all of them acknowledge the greatness of Palmerston and speak with awe of that dramatic stroke by which he captured Acre, drove the victorious army of a rebellious pasha back on Egypt, and restored Syria and Palestine to the Sultan of Turkey. This feat is described as worthy of Chatham 'for bold conception and brilliant performance.' 'The expulsion of the Egyptians from Turkey remains a great monument alike of diplomatic skill and administrative energy.' Thirty years later the novelist was in a position to rival the feat of statesmanship he had praised. He overruled his own Cabinet, overcame popular opposition, and sent the British fleet to the Bosphorus. He kept the Russians out of Constantinople, compelled the victors to rewrite their treaty and induced the vanquished to hand over Cyprus to Victoria—whom he had already presented with an Imperial Crown. A cool judgment will question the policy of this dramatic intervention and deplore the mistakes made at the Congress of Berlin, but it is hard to exaggerate the daring and courage of Disraeli.

Lord Salisbury is the last Victorian to leave a deep and permanent mark on foreign policy. As a young man he had publicly criticised the diplomacy of Palmerston and Russell with as much bitterness as ability. He had been with Disraeli at the Congress, and brought 'Peace with Honour' back with him from Berlin. His knowledge was greater than his chief's. He saw that the settlement was no true settlement, and in later years did what he could to remedy its defects. He worked silently, for he was by nature reserved, and an unhappy incident had taught him the dangers of premature leakage of diplomatic secrets to the press. And it was here, I think, that he erred. Castlereagh had aroused suspicion when he kept the secrets of diplomacy from the public, and it was too late to imitate Castlereagh in the eighties. But his diplomacy was firm and resolute, though he seldom invited public opinion to share his confidences. In his later years he failed, I think, to see the new tendencies of the future. Europe was no longer a chaos of atoms, it was grouped in two Leagues. A Triple Alliance of Central European States had been created by Bismarck, and a Dual or Franco-Russian Alliance had arisen in reply to it. Evidently it had become harder for England to stand by itself. What would happen if both Alliances combined against us? The younger generation—men like Chamberlain and Lord Lansdowne—declared that our isolation was not 'splendid' but dangerous. They wished Allies to be found somewhere. In 1898 Salisbury approached Russia, and Chamberlain approached Germany. Both overtures failed, and then the South African War came. Our isolation was revealed by the storm which assailed us from the Press of the Continent. It looked too as if there might be something behind the pens of the writers as if France, Germany and Russia might unite their arms against us. And though the danger passed, the cloud remained.

So in 1901 Germany and England again discussed the possibility of an Alliance. It failed and (as we know) England abandoned Germany and looked elsewhere. Though he lived to see the Japanese Alliance, Lord Salisbury had finished his course. And his political testament may be found in his memorandum on the Anglo-German negotiation of 1901, a paper which contributed to its failure[1]. It shews distrust of public opinion in England, and a belief that no treaty of alliance would be endorsed by it. It shews an unabated confidence in England's ability to stand alone. Except under Napoleon isolation was a danger, which we had never felt practically and 'in whose existence we have no historical reason for believing.' His colleagues did not adopt his views at any rate as to the present and the result was an alliance in Asia and an Entente in Europe, which carried with them immeasurable consequences. But Lord Salisbury himself remained to the last a statesman of the Victorian school, proud of England's isolation and still confident of her safety,

1 The text is in Gooch and Temperley, *British Documents on the Origin of the War* [1927], II. 68–9.

though the clouds were gathering darkly around him.

To sum up the diplomatic life of the reign—I would say that our foreign policy leaned on England too much and on Europe too little. Castlereagh's European dream had been a splendid failure, and Canning had been great enough to see that neither his English nor any policy could endure for ever. New facts and unforeseen cases might change any system. He warned his ambassadors 'not to lay down beforehand fixed resolutions for eventual probabilities.' His warnings were forgotten and his English policy imitated and exaggerated by his successors. The reactions towards a European policy were few and, when they came, too violent or too evanescent to produce much effect. The last two great leaders allowed England still to be, what she could no longer be with safety, alone in Europe.

There were certainly periods in this age when isolation was right and no European policy possible. But there were others when insularity was a mistake, and when sympathetic attempts to understand and to work with Europe might have resulted in permanent good.

VIII

If we sum up the age what do we find? Great men certainly, even within our narrow limits, men great both in deeds and character. Not perhaps in war, for Wellington was an august survival from another age, and the only man of his stature in this one, though Anglo-Saxon, was not an Englishman, the gallant Lee of Virginia. In my other categories —there are so many great names shining on the scroll, that there has not even been time to mention them all. Who, for instance, could deny greatness to Stratford de Redcliffe—the 'voice of

England in the East,' to Randolph Churchill, the most original of politicians, or to half-a-dozen Indian and Colonial rulers? And we could marshal great and splendid names among social workers, missionaries, travellers as well.

There is no doubt of the men—what then of the age? It has been the fashion to sneer at its complacency—to say that it mistook material ease for civilisation and mechanical for moral progress. These charges may be true but they do not give us the whole truth. Two main tendencies characterise the age, and these tendencies were usually in conflict. The first tendency was the spirit of compromise, the spirit of order and of decency, so dear to the middle class, the class then articulate and politically self-conscious. Its political instinct was sure though not infallible. It failed to guarantee our safety in time of peace at the beginning of the reign and to give us efficiency in war at its end. In diplomacy it deferred too much to its leaders and followed too selfish a policy, looking only to immediate needs. But the problems of giving self-government and self-defence to the colonies were solved with just that practical good sense and in just that spirit of cautious innovation, which the middle class impressed upon their rulers. Look at one great crisis of the age at home, the crisis which ended Protection and established Free Trade. Was this accomplished by any one man? Sir Robert Peel is the answer. But was it really accomplished by Sir Robert? His policy for years shewed an experimental yet definite approach to Free Trade, until the moment arrived when he thought it necessary and right to carry it and he did so. He divided his party and lost his power, but he had exactly expressed the feeling of the dominant class in the country. Here again we seem to see that the class was wiser and stronger than any man or any combination of parties. Take again the case of Gladstone. He balances the accounts of the nation as neatly and precisely as a grocer adds up his weekly bills, and though an advanced politician of the time is also the favourite of the City. Do we not see here how exactly the spirit of the age has fashioned even greatness in its pattern? Take another movement. The transition to democracy in Europe has usually been accompanied with revolution and violence. In England it scarcely ruffled the surfaces and caused nothing but a demonstration in Hyde Park. Our leaders seem not to have known when to refuse, or when to offer, an extension of the franchise. But the middle class knew and, as soon as they thought it desirable, they obtained their desire.

The second tendency of the age and of the ruling class, was exactly in conflict with the first. There was a tendency to reject all compromise, a tendency to ruthless logic, and to a mechanical perfection and rigidity of thought. The political ideas of Bentham and Herbert Spencer, the economic doctrines of *laisser faire* and of free trade, of self help and free enterprise will illustrate what I mean. How earnestly these advocates pressed their views, how they scorned their opponents, how strongly they stood by the Eternal Verities. And the utterances are sometimes as ruthless as the theories. How revolutionary were some reputable citizens, when they denounced the wickedness of Kings and of Emperors in 1848, or the cruelty of the slave owners to whom all compensation should be refused. And there is a depth of sympathy with the poor in the writings of so many, of Charles Reade or of Disraeli and even in the earlier pages of *Punch*, which makes us wonder if the age was so callous or cautious after all. Its most popular author was Dickens, and who was more relentless in his attack on social evils, or more passionate in his indignation against them? And are not these rebels just as characteristic of the age as Gladstone or Peel? Indeed I could not bid you to study any politics or send you to any history so rich in revelation as the novels of Dickens. They diffuse that atmosphere which is lost among protocols and parliamentary debates, they contain that essence of which politics is only the shell. His world is a truly Victorian world—in which myriads of characters crowd the stage, every one of them different, every one stamped with the mind of their creator. That is the middle class in the reign of Victoria, a medley, with and without, a purpose; a crowd now following, now controlling, its leaders.

Printed in the United States
By Bookmasters